Text and illustrations Copyright © 2020 Franziska Wenzel

First published by Luna Press Publishing, Edinburgh, 2020

Imaginarium ©2020. All rights reserved. No part of this publication may be reproduced, stored in a retrieval system, or transmitted in any form or by any means, electronic, mechanical, photocopy, recording or otherwise, without prior written permission of the copyright owners. Nor can it be circulated in any form of binding or cover other than that in which it is published and without similar condition including this condition being imposed on a subsequent purchaser.

www.lunapresspublishing.com

ISBN-13: 978-1-911143-99-4.

"For everyone's endless patience"

WELCOME TO MY WORLDS...

Thank you for purchasing this book and supporting
Luna Press Publishing and our authors.
Please consider leaving a review.

Explore our store at www.lunapresspublishing.com

www.ingramcontent.com/pod-product-compliance
Lightning Source LLC
Chambersburg PA
CBHW042032100526
44587CB00029B/4386